W9-CNQ-224

CALIFORNIA

Past and Present

Laura La Bella

rosen publishing's
rosen
central®

New York

To North Miles Kilian: Dream Big

Published in 2010 by The Rosen Publishing Group, Inc.
29 East 21st Street, New York, NY 10010

First Edition

Library of Congress Cataloging-in-Publication Data

La Bella, Laura.
California: past and present / Laura La Bella.—1st ed.
    p. cm.—(The United States: past and present)
Includes bibliographical references and index.
ISBN-13: 978-1-4358-5290-7 (library binding)
ISBN-13: 978-1-4358-5578-6 (pbk)
ISBN-13: 978-1-4358-5579-3 (6 pack)
1. California—Juvenile literature. I. Title.
F861.3.L26 2010
979.4—dc22

                                                        2008055151

Manufactured in the United States of America

On the cover: Top left: A "miner forty-niner" pans for gold during the California gold rush. Top right: High-tech research and manufacturing fuels Silicon Valley, one of California's strongest economic engines. Bottom: The Golden Gate Bridge spans San Francisco Bay, connecting San Francisco and Marin County.

Contents

Introduction   5

Chapter 1
The Geography of California   6

Chapter 2
The History of California   13

Chapter 3
The Government of California   20

Chapter 4
The Economy of California   25

Chapter 5
**People from California:
Past and Present**   30

Timeline   38

California at a Glance   39

Glossary   41

For More Information   42

For Further Reading   44

Bibliography   44

Index   46

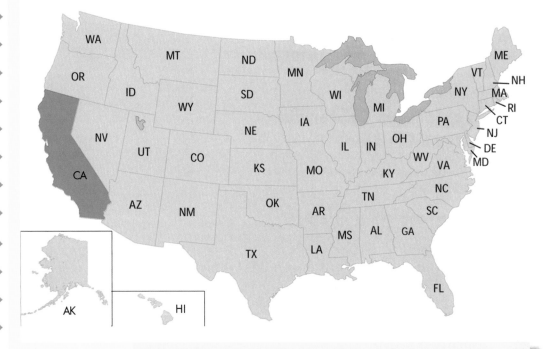

California was admitted to the United States on September 9, 1850. The third-largest state in terms of geographical size, California is also the most populous.

Introduction

California is rich in history, legend, and fairy tale. When gold was first discovered there, tens of thousands of people flocked to the state, believing in a dream. Legendary figures in history like Wyatt Earp policed the West, and Howard Hughes redefined air travel there. It's the place where fairy tales, from Harry Potter to Cinderella, come true on the silver screens of Hollywood.

In California, you will find towering redwood forests, where Sequoia trees reach more than 370 feet (113 meters) into the sky. The state's Central Valley is one of the country's most productive agricultural centers. The majestic Sierra Nevada mountain range, gleaming deserts, and world-renowned cities add personality and distinction to one of the largest states in the United States.

California has also become a center of technology and industry. Silicon Valley and Palo Alto are hubs for software development, gaming, computing, and technology. A number of innovative companies, from Google and eBay to Apple and Hewlett-Packard, have established their headquarters there.

The state's people are just as diverse as its geography and industries. The population is a melting pot of cultures and traditions from around the world. It's the most multicultural state in the country, boasting the highest number of Native Americans, Hispanic Americans, and Asian Americas in the United States.

For these reasons, there is a lot to discover in California.

Chapter 1

THE GEOGRAPHY OF CALIFORNIA

California is located on the West Coast of the United States. It borders the Pacific Ocean on the west, while its northern state line borders Oregon. The eastern side of the state borders Nevada and Arizona. Its southern edge borders the Mexican state of Baja California, which is the northernmost province of the country of Mexico.

With an area of 163,696 square miles (423,971 square kilometers), California is the third-largest state in the United States in terms of geographic area. Only Alaska and Texas are bigger. The state's estimated population in 2007 was more than 36.5 million, the most of any state in the country.

With such a huge population, California contains some of the nation's largest cities. In fact, of the fifty most populous U.S. cities, eight are located in California. The eight are: Fresno, Long Beach, Los Angeles, San Diego, San Francisco, San Jose, Sacramento, and Oakland.

Mountains

The state of California has a varied geography, as well as a diverse climate. There is a wide range of major cities, rugged mountains,

Los Angeles's Chinatown is a bustling cultural district and a vivid example of California's diverse population. The state is home to the largest Asian American population in the United States.

scenic valleys, large lakes, dry deserts, and frigid glaciers. And there's a beautiful coastline.

California has three significant mountain ranges: the Cascade Range, the California White Mountains, and the Sierra Nevada. These mountain ranges contain several notable geographical features, including:

- Lake Tahoe, a large and clear freshwater lake in the northern Sierra Nevada.

- Yosemite National Park, which is filled with stunning waterfalls and granite domes.
- Mount Whitney, at 14,505 feet (4,421 m), marks the highest point in the contiguous United States (the lower forty-eight states).
- Three groves of giant sequoias, the world's largest, tallest, and longest-living trees.

Valleys

From the dizzying heights of some of the most beautiful mountain ranges to the profound depths of its canyons, California features some stunning valleys. The Central Valley is a large, flat valley that dominates the central portion of California. It is home to much of the state's agricultural industry. The valley stretches nearly 400 miles (644 km) from north to south. Its northern half is referred to as the Sacramento Valley and its southern half as the San Joaquin Valley. Yosemite Valley is a world-famous scenic location in the Sierra Nevada. It is the centerpiece of Yosemite National Park and attracts visitors from all parts of the world.

Lakes and Rivers

With a state as large as California, there are several major bodies of water and prominent rivers. Lake Tahoe is a large freshwater lake in the Sierra Nevada mountains. It is the second-deepest lake in the country and the area has become a major tourist attraction for skiing and outdoor recreational activities. Many people are also drawn to the nearby casinos in Reno, a city built on the Nevada shores of Lake Tahoe.

California boasts a range of geographical features, from snowy mountains to warm beaches. Emerald Bay, shown here, is located at Lake Tahoe.

Clear Lake, believed to be one of the oldest lakes in North America, is a geological fluke. The lake sits on a huge block of stone that tilts to the north at the same degree at which the lake fills in with sediment. The lake's odd positioning keeps the water at roughly the same depth at all times, regardless of rainfall amounts.

The two most prominent rivers within California are the Sacramento River and the San Joaquin River, which drain the Central Valley and flow to the Pacific Ocean through the San Francisco Bay. Two other important rivers are the Klamath River, in the north, and the Colorado River, on the southeast border.

The City of the Angels

The city of Los Angeles began as a tiny Spanish mission founded by a Franciscan friar in 1771. The religious settlement gradually evolved into a tiny town, or pueblo, composed mostly of Mexican ranchers. The pueblo continued to exist after Mexico gained independence from Spain and took control of California. In 1847, following the Mexican-American War, the United States won California. The little Spanish pueblo began to grow in population—thanks to the influx of settlers in the wake of the gold rush and the completion of the Southern Pacific train line, which terminated in Los Angeles. When oil was discovered in 1892, the city became a center of oil production and its population swelled further.

By the beginning of the twentieth century, Los Angeles had a population of around one hundred thousand, a significant railway system, and a growing renown for its aircraft manufacturing industry. Douglas Aircraft Company (which later became McDonnell Douglas and eventually merged with Boeing) began building planes, leading to an influx of highly educated workers who moved to the L.A. area seeking work. During World War II, Los Angeles became a major center for the production of aircraft, war supplies, and ammunition. Today, the city of Los Angeles has more than 3.6 million residents. And the greater Los Angeles area, including Los Angeles County, has more than 9.8 million residents.

This is the earliest known image of Los Angeles. What began as a small Spanish settlement has grown into the largest city in California.

Deserts and Glaciers

Fresh water is a crucial and significant part of California, its economy, its livability, and its culture. Yet the state also has deserts. The most famous one is the Mojave Desert. The Mojave Desert experiences dramatic temperature extremes and has four distinct seasons. The winter months bring temperatures that dip to below 20 degrees Fahrenheit (-7 degrees Celsius). Storms can bring large amounts of rainfall and snowfall. In the sum-

This is Death Valley National Park. In 1913, it recorded the highest temperature ever in the Western Hemisphere at 134°F (56.6°C).

mer, Death Valley, located in the Mojave Desert, is the hottest point in North America. It is also the lowest point in the country. Temperatures there can reach between 120 and 130°F (49 and 54°C).

On the opposite end of the spectrum, California also has several major glaciers. The largest, Palisade Glacier in the Sierra Nevada, was formed only seven hundred years ago during the so-called

Little Ice Age. It is a large, slow-moving mass of ice composed of compacted layers of snow.

Plants and Animals

In the midst of California's many ecosystems exists a bewildering number of plant and animal species. Some of the most notable animals include salmon, steelheads, trout, elk, pronghorns, deer, bighorn sheep, wild pigs, bears, wolverines, beavers, foxes, otters, sea turtles, tortoises, sea lions, seals, whales, assorted waterfowl, grouse, wild turkeys, quail, albatrosses, cranes, pelicans, hawks, eagles, condors, and owls.

Some of the state's most distinctive vegetation includes redwoods, Indian paintbrushes, various kinds of thistle, cypresses, larkspurs, cacti, evening primroses, mariposa lilies, manzanitas, spineflowers, dudleyas, sagebrush bluebells, buckwheat, daisies, honeysuckles, morning glories, ladyslippers, firs, fiddlenecks, lichens, mosses, milk vetches, sedges, and various kinds of wild grasses.

Chapter 2

THE HISTORY OF CALIFORNIA

The area now known as California was at one time inhabited by more than seventy distinct groups of Native Americans. Most made their home in one of two places. There were large, settled populations living on the coast. They hunted sea mammals, fished for salmon, and gathered shellfish. And there were similar populations of Native Americans living inland. These groups hunted wild game, such as deer and elk, and they gathered nuts, acorns, and berries.

The first European to explore the coast was a Portuguese sailor named João Rodrigues Cabrilho. He visited the area in 1542, while sailing for the Spanish Empire. About thirty-seven years later, the English explorer Francis Drake navigated the coastal areas. Drake claimed an undefined portion of the California coast in 1579. In the late 1700s, Spanish missionaries began to establish themselves in what is now San Diego. The Spanish continued to rule this area, as well as Mexico, until 1821, when the Mexican War of Independence gave Mexico (which then included California) independence from Spain. For the next twenty-five years, "Alta California"—which consisted of California and most of present-day Arizona—remained a remote northern province of Mexico.

The War for Water

Mission Santa Barbara was founded on December 4, 1786, and still functions as a church today.

As more people moved to California following the U.S. takeover of the territory after the Mexican-American War in 1847 and the gold rush of 1849, new methods of transportation were developed. Steamships began regular service from San Francisco, and the first transcontinental railroad was established. The line's completion united California with the central and eastern portions of the United States. It also made travel faster. It used to take weeks, or even months, to get from California to the East Coast. Now, it took only a few days. The settling of California completed the dream of Manifest Destiny, which was the American belief that U.S. territorial control should stretch from coast to coast.

The opening up of this frontier also allowed for the newly settled land to be farmed and used for grazing. Agriculture and livestock, California's major "boom growth" fields after the gold rush, were established. This growth in population and homesteading led to some conflicts. This included a water war between farmers and ranchers near Owens Valley and the rapidly growing city of Los Angeles, which was developed in a dry area in Southern California.

The California Water Wars began when Frederick Eaton was elected mayor of Los Angeles in 1898. He and William Mulholland, the superintendent of the newly created Los Angeles Department of Water and Power, wanted the city to become a major hub of the American West. The only factor limiting Los Angeles's growth was its lack of a water supply. Eaton and Mulholland realized that Owens Valley had a large amount of runoff from the Sierra Nevada. An aqueduct could deliver water from the valley to Los Angeles. The 233-mile (375 km) Los Angeles Aqueduct was built to divert water from Owens Valley to Los Angeles. So much water was taken from the ordinarily fertile valley that it eventually became dry and useless for agriculture.

The California Aqueduct is a 443-mile (713 km) channel that carries water from the north of the state to Southern California.

From Gold to Silver

In the wake of California's frenzied quest for gold came a new dream-like, money-making pursuit. This one involved silver . . . the "silver

From Gold Rush to Golden State: California's Population Boom

The discovery of gold at Sutter's Mill, California, on January 24, 1848, unleashed the largest migration of people in the United States. At first, word spread slowly about the discovery. But by the beginning of 1849, word of the gold rush had reached the East Coast and was spreading around the world. An overwhelming number of gold seekers—often called "forty-niners," for the year they arrived in California—began to descend on the area from virtually every continent. Tens of thousands of people flooded the state.

The effects of the gold rush were substantial. Between 1847 and 1870, the population of San Francisco exploded. The formerly tiny hamlet of 500 settlers living in tents was quickly transformed into a boomtown of more than 150,000 people. The entire state's population tripled from the beginning of the gold rush in 1847 to its end, around 1860. This population boom led to roads, churches, and schools being built. And it transformed small villages throughout California into major towns and thriving cities. A system of territorial laws and a government were created, and representatives traveled to Washington, D.C., where they applied for statehood. California entered the Union and became the thirty-first state in 1850. Today, California's estimated population is more than 36.5 million people, the most of any state in the country.

screen" to be more precise. In early 1910, director D. W. Griffith filmed the first movie ever shot in "Hollywoodland," a district in Los Angeles that would eventually become known simply as Hollywood. The movie, appropriately enough, was called *In Old California*. The first studio in Hollywood was established by the New Jersey–based Centaur Company, which wanted to make Westerns in scenery-rich California.

The first few decades of the twentieth century saw the rise of the Hollywood studio system. MGM, Universal, and Warner Brothers all acquired land in Hollywood. Soon, other production and movie companies began to establish themselves in Hollywood as well. By 1915, the majority of all movies made in the United States were produced in the Los Angeles area. In the 1940s, television stations began setting up affiliates in California. And in the 1950s, music and recording studios began moving there, too. Hollywood had become the capital of the entertainment industry by the 1960s. Today, the cities of Los Angeles and Burbank are still the headquarters of the American entertainment industry.

The "Hollywood" sign originally advertised a new housing development in the Hollywood Hills. It became a symbol of the U.S. movie industry.

The Reagan Years and Campus Unrest

In the 1930s, a young man named Ronald Reagan traveled from Illinois to Hollywood to become an actor. After a successful movie career, in which he made more than seventy-seven films, he was elected governor of California in 1967. During his two terms, Reagan

Former Hollywood actor Ronald Reagan was governor of California before being elected the fortieth president of the United States.

became involved in several high-profile conflicts with the student protest movements of the era. There were numerous demonstrations and strikes, many of which were held on the campus of the University of California at Berkeley.

Reagan was displeased with the university administration for its tolerance of student antiwar demonstrations. On May 15, 1969, during one campus protest, a major confrontation ensued between law enforcement officials and the crowd of young demonstrators. Reagan ordered the California Highway Patrol and other officers to quell the protests in an incident that became known as Bloody Thursday. During the incident, hundreds of students and Berkeley residents were injured. Reagan sent 2,200 state National Guard troops to occupy the city of Berkeley for two weeks in order to crack down on the protesters. He defended his actions by saying, "If it takes a bloodbath, let's get it over with. No more appeasement."

In 1981, Reagan became the fortieth president of the United States. His time in the Oval Office was nearly as turbulent as his two terms as governor of California. His presidency coincided with a tumultuous time in American history. The Cold War was at its peak, the economy was struggling, the AIDS crisis was beginning to emerge and wreak havoc, and the nation was involved in an ongoing, expensive, and controversial war on drugs.

California's Cutting-Edge Social Trends

California is well known for being a leader in cutting-edge social and legislative trends. During the 1960s, its government became more liberal and progressive, emphasizing the rights of criminal defendants even as the crime rate soared. The state was the first to create strict product liability laws protecting consumers from tainted, faulty, or malfunctioning products. It also allowed people to sue for damages associated with the "negligent infliction of emotional distress." In other words, people could receive money for the harmful emotional results of an accident or crime.

Also beginning in the 1960s, California became a leader in family law. It was the first state to allow for no-fault divorce, in which a couple can divorce without having to prove wrongdoing on the part of either spouse. In 2002, the state legislature granted registered domestic partners the same rights under state law as married spouses. In 2008, California became only the second state in the Union to legalize same-sex marriage when its supreme court ruled the ban against it to be unconstitutional. However, this law was later overturned by a voter proposition in November 2008.

Chapter 3

THE GOVERNMENT OF CALIFORNIA

The state of California, with Sacramento as its capital, is governed as a republic. It has three branches: the executive, the legislative, and the judicial.

The executive branch consists of the governor and independently elected constitutional officers. Arnold Schwarzenegger, a Republican and former action movie star, became governor of the state in 2003. Schwarzenegger, who was born in Austria, appeared in more than forty films, including the popular *Terminator* series. The governor has a number of powers and responsibilities. He can sign or veto laws passed by the legislature, propose a state budget, give the annual State of the State address, and grant pardons for any crime.

The legislative branch consists of an eighty-member state assembly and a forty-member state senate. The main responsibility of the state representatives is to introduce bills and vote on them to decide whether or not they become state law.

The judicial branch of the California state government consists of the supreme court of California and the lower courts. California's judiciary system is the largest in the United States. It has a total of 1,600 judges. The state's judicial system is overseen by state supreme court justices.

In addition, the interests of California are represented in the U.S. Congress. Like all states in the nation, California is represented by two senators in the U.S. Senate. However, it has dozens of representatives in the House of Representatives.

California has fifty-three congressional representatives. One of its most well-known representatives is Nancy Pelosi, who served as Speaker of the House in the 2000s. In this position, Pelosi was the presiding officer of the House. She was the first female Speaker of the House in U.S. history. Pelosi was second in the presidential line of succession, after the vice president, in the event of a crisis that temporarily or permanently made the president unable to serve. This means if something were to happen to both the president and the vice president, Pelosi would take their place as leader of the country.

Arnold Schwarzenegger starred in *The Terminator* and *Total Recall*. He became governor of California in 2003.

California's Political Influence

Before the gold rush, California was a freewheeling frontier comprised of small mining camps scattered across largely ungoverned territory. After the gold rush, California quickly became the thirty-first state in the Union. As its population grew, the state gained more and more seats in the U.S. House of Representatives—and more and more political influence. The number of congressional representatives that a state has is based on its population. Today, California's fifty-three congressional representatives are the most of any state in the country.

Also based on population is the number of electoral votes assigned to each state. Electoral votes determine the president and vice president of the United States. They are equal to the number of senators and representatives that each state has in Congress. California currently has fifty-five electoral votes, which makes it a highly sought-after state during presidential elections.

Progressive Politics and Ballot Initiatives

California is known for having a liberal and progressive political culture. The state has supported domestic partnerships for gays and lesbians. It has also taken a leadership role in the fight toward saving the environment. Before any other state, California established renewable energy programs and has been proactive in helping offset climate change caused by environmental factors.

California's citizens can propose, overturn, or amend a law in the state's constitution by using a ballot proposition. This process gives voters a more direct voice in their state government.

California is one of the few states whose citizens can overturn a law or amend the state's constitution. A ballot proposition is a method of amending state law through what is called the initiative and referendum process. State laws may be proposed directly by the public. The state's constitution may be amended either by public petition or by the legislature submitting a proposed constitutional amendment to the electorate (state voters). The process of allowing the public to propose legislation or constitutional amendments is called the initiative. A referendum is the process by which the state legislature proposes constitutional amendments. This process can occur in one of two ways.

First, the California legislature may pass an act, which is signed by the governor, proposing a state constitutional amendment. The amendment is then submitted to the voters as a referendum at the next statewide election. If more than 50 percent of the voters approve the referendum, the constitutional amendment is approved and goes into effect.

The second way for a law to change is if the general public suggests either an amendment to the state constitution or the creation of new statute laws. This is done by writing a proposed constitutional amendment or statute as a petition and submitting the petition to the California attorney general. The petition must be signed by a certain number of registered voters.

An Increasingly Blue State

California politics have consistently leaned toward the Democratic Party, especially in recent years. This tendency is most obvious in presidential elections. California has the most electoral votes of any state in the nation. It has fifty-five electoral votes and is poised to gain another three due to population growth. Democratic candidates for U.S. Senate seats have easily won every Senate race since 1992, and they have maintained consistent majorities in both houses of the state legislature.

Chapter 4

THE ECONOMY OF CALIFORNIA

California's economy ranks among the ten largest economies in the world. Among the largest industries in California are entertainment, agriculture, high technology, and wine production.

That's Entertainment!

The U.S. entertainment industry is based in Hollywood. The very first motion picture was filmed there in 1910. By 1947, the first commercial television station west of the Mississippi River, KTLA, began operating in Hollywood. Today, all three major television networks—ABC, CBS, and NBC—have studios and production facilities in Hollywood and the greater Los Angeles area. Major recording studios are located in Los Angeles, as are the West Coast offices of major magazines.

Seeds of Growth

California is the nation's top agricultural state. Its agriculture industry generates approximately $31.8 billion a year, more than that of any other state. California produces more than 350 crops, including many that are not grown on a large scale anywhere else in the United States. These include almonds, artichokes, figs, olives, persimmons,

Most American movies and TV shows are shot in Hollywood, including at Universal Studios *(above)*.

pomegranates, prunes, raisins, and walnuts. The state grows more than half of the nation's fruits and vegetables.

The hub of California's agricultural efforts is the Central Valley. Approximately 6.5 million people live in the Central Valley. The Central Valley is one of the most productive agricultural regions on the planet and is commonly referred to as the "Fruit Basket of the World." The state's top-ten commodities include milk and cream, grapes, nursery products, almonds, cattle and calves, lettuce, strawberries, tomatoes, hay, and flowers.

Silicon Valley

Silicon Valley, located in the southern part of the San Francisco Bay area, has long been known as the global center for the development of computers and high technology. The term "Silicon Valley" originally referred to the region's large number of silicon chip innovators and manufacturers. Eventually, the term came to refer to all of the high-tech businesses in the area.

Silicon Valley has been most renowned in recent years for innovations in software and Internet services. The companies there have significantly influenced computer operating systems and software.

The Golden Age of Hollywood

There were eight major film studios during the Golden Age of Hollywood, which lasted from the late 1920s silent era to the late 1950s. These studios were Columbia Pictures, 20th Century-Fox, Warner Brothers, Paramount, Universal Pictures, Metro-Goldwyn-Mayer (MGM), United Artists, and RKO. Most Hollywood films adhered closely to one of five different genres: Westerns; slapstick, "screwball," or romantic comedies; musicals; animated cartoons; and biographies. The studios often featured a stable roster of directors, actors, and other creative artists who worked under long-term contracts.

Today, after a series of mergers and closings, six conglomerates—Time Warner, Viacom, the Walt Disney Company, Sony, General Electric/Vivendi, and News Corporation—put out nearly all American films. These corporations operate a number of studios—including Miramax, Fox Searchlight, and Paramount—as divisions within the larger parent companies. Instead of studios signing creative teams to long-term contracts, many producers, actors, and directors now have independent production companies. These companies shop film scripts or movie ideas around to different studios, which have the option of purchasing an idea or passing on it.

One of the region's major success stories is Hewlett-Packard, which specializes in developing and manufacturing computing, storage, and networking hardware, software, and services. It may be the largest technology company in the world, but it had rather humble beginnings. In 1939, William Hewlett and David Packard founded the company in Packard's garage in Palo Alto, which became the center of Silicon Valley.

Google is located in Silicon Valley. The term "Silicon Valley" first referred to the region's many silicon chip makers.

Thousands of high-tech companies are headquartered in Silicon Valley. Among the most recognized are Adobe Systems, Apple, eBay, Facebook, Google, Hewlett-Packard, Intel, and Yahoo!

Wine Country

California is also famous for producing some of the world's best wines. The state accounts for nearly 90 percent of U.S. wine production. The gold rush brought waves of new settlers to the region, increasing the population and the local demand for wine.

The growing wine industry took hold in northern California, centering on the counties of Sonoma and Napa. The climate in this part of the state is perfect for growing grapes. The Pacific Ocean, along with large bays like the San Francisco Bay, helps moderate temperatures and climate in the region. They provide cool winds and fog that balance the intense heat and sunshine typical of inland areas in northern California. And with mild winters, there is little threat of frost, snow, or sleet causing significant damage.

During the gold rush, some of California's oldest wineries— including Buena Vista Winery, Charles Krug Winery, Inglenook Winery, and Schramsberg Vineyard—were founded. Today, Napa Valley, Sonoma Valley, and the Southern California communities of

Santa Barbara, Temecula Valley, and Paso Robles are major producers of wine.

Oil Production

California has more than a dozen of the largest oil fields in the country, including the Midway-Sunset Oil Field, which is the second-largest oil field in the contiguous United States. California's hydroelectric power potential ranks second nationwide, after the state of Washing-

More than four hundred wineries operate in the California counties of Sonoma and Napa, known worldwide for premium grape-growing.

ton. Substantial geothermal and wind power resources are found along the coastal mountain ranges and the eastern border shared with Nevada.

While California is the most populous state in the nation, it ranks second (behind Texas) in its demand for energy. The state has one of the lowest per capita (per person) energy consumption rates in the country. This is in spite of the fact that more motor vehicles are registered in California than in any other state, and worker commute times are among the longest in the country.

Chapter 5

PEOPLE FROM CALIFORNIA: PAST AND PRESENT

With an area of 163,696 square miles (423,971 square km), California is the third-largest state in the country in terms of geographic area. In terms of population, however, California rules. The state's estimated population in 2007 was more than 36.5 million, the most of any state in the country.

Not only is California's population large, it's also diverse. It has the largest minority population in the country, making up 57 percent of the total state population. Its population is 58.9 percent Caucasian (white), 35.9 percent Hispanic, 12.3 percent Asian American, 6.2 percent African American, 3.3 percent mixed ethnicities, and 0.7 Native American. The fifth-largest population of African Americans lives in the state, and approximately one-third of the nation's entire Asian population—nearly 4.5 million people—call California home. The state also has the largest Native American population—more than 376,000—of any state in the country.

With such a diverse population, it shouldn't be surprising to learn that there are a variety of languages spoken by the state's residents. While the majority speak English, visitors will hear many other languages. Spanish and Filipino are very common, as are Korean, Vietnamese, and the Chinese dialects of Cantonese and Mandarin.

California's Celebrity Citizens

Actors and actresses, political leaders, sports figures, and accomplished scientists: California has a rich history of famous people who were born and raised in the state or who have had significant influence over the state's development.

Entertainment and Literature

George Lucas (1944–)
George Lucas is the creator of the epic space saga *Star Wars*. He also introduced the archaeologist-adventurer Indiana Jones (portrayed by actor Harrison Ford), who has been featured in four blockbuster films. Born in Modesto, Lucas is one of the film industry's most financially successful independent directors/producers. He has his own studio, LucasFilm; sound and visual effects companies, Skywalker Sound and Industrial Light & Magic; and Lucas Arts, a highly regarded gaming company.

George Lucas, who was born in Modesto, is the creator of *Star Wars*, the third-highest-grossing film series in history.

31

The Hearst Media Empire

William Randolph Hearst (1863–1951) was a newspaper magnate and leading newspaper publisher. While a student at Harvard University, his father, George Hearst, had acquired the *San Francisco Examiner*. Hearst took over the paper from his father, and it became the most respected and influential paper in the San Francisco area. Hearst opened newspapers in other cities, including Chicago, Los Angeles, and Boston.

By the mid-1920s, Hearst had built a nationwide string of twenty-eight newspapers, among them the *Los Angeles Examiner*, the *Boston American*, the *Atlanta Georgian*, the *Chicago Examiner*, the *Detroit Times*, the *Seattle Post-Intelligencer*, the *Washington Times*, and the *Washington Herald*. Interested in expanding his publishing empire even further, Hearst got into book publishing and magazines.

Today, the Hearst Corporation is one of the largest communications companies in the world. It owns sixteen daily newspapers and forty-nine weekly newspapers, nearly two hundred magazines from around the world, and twenty-eight television stations. It is also involved in business publishing, Internet businesses, television production, newspaper features distribution, and real estate.

Robert Redford (1936–) Robert Redford is an Academy Award–winning actor, director, and producer. Born in Santa Monica, Redford has appeared in more than sixty films and has directed seven. In 1978, he founded the Sundance Film Festival, which caters to independent filmmakers in the United States and has received recognition from the industry as an excellent place to debut films and attract distributors for them.

John Steinbeck (1902–1968) John Steinbeck was a Pulitzer Prize– and Noble Prize–winning writer. He is best known for writing *The Grapes of Wrath* and *Of Mice and Men*, both published in the mid-1930s. Born in Salinas Valley, Steinbeck wrote twenty-five books, including sixteen novels, six nonfiction books, and several collections of short stories. In 1962, he received the Nobel Prize for Literature.

Shirley Temple Black (1928–) Shirley Temple Black is the most famous child star in film history. She appeared in more than sixty films and won an Academy Award before leaving Hollywood to become a U.S. ambassador and a diplomat.

Politics, Government, and the Military

Richard M. Nixon (1913–1994)

Richard Nixon was the thirty-seventh president of the United States and was the only president ever to resign from office. Born in Yorba Linda, Nixon was a congressman and a U.S. senator before he was elected to the presidency. As president, he successfully negotiated a cease-fire that ended the Vietnam War.

Nixon's resignation from the presidency was the result of the Watergate scandal. The scandal began with the arrest of five men who broke into the Democratic National

Richard Nixon, from Yorba Linda, was the only U.S. president to resign from office.

Committee headquarters at the Watergate Office complex in Washington, D.C., on June 17, 1972. Investigations conducted by the Federal Bureau of Investigation (FBI) and other investigative committees found that the burglary was one of several illegal activities authorized and carried out by Nixon's staff. Facing impeachment and conviction for his role in the Watergate break-in and subsequent cover-up, Nixon resigned from office.

George S. Patton (1885–1945) George Patton was born in San Gabril Township. He became a distinguished U.S. Army officer, rising to the rank of general. Patton was a major figure in World War II, helping to successfully lead the invasion of Normandy and the Battle of the Bulge.

Sports

Jeff Gordon (1971–) Jeff Gordon is a professional race car driver for the National Association for Stock Car Auto Racing, or NASCAR. Born in Vallejo, Gordon is a four-time champion of the NASCAR Sprint Series (formerly the Winston Cup) and is a three-time winner of the Daytona 500.

Joe DiMaggio (1914–1999) Joe DiMaggio, one of the most famous players in baseball history, was born in Martinez. He played for the New York Yankees, leading the team to nine World Series titles in thirteen years. A member of the Baseball Hall of Fame, DiMaggio was a three-time MVP winner and a thirteen-time All-Star. He was the only player to be selected for the All-Star Game every season he played. At the time of his retirement in 1951, he had the fifth-most career home runs (361) and the sixth-highest slugging percentage (.579) in baseball history.

Venus and Serena Williams (1980– and 1981–) Venus and Serena Williams are professional tennis champions who also happen to be sisters. Although they were born in Michigan, they grew up in Compton, California, a tough city known for its high levels of poverty and crime. The sisters began playing tennis, and both joined the professional circuit as teenagers. Serena has won twenty-eight singles championships, eleven doubles championships, and the gold medal at the 2000 Olympics. Venus has thirty-nine career titles, including sixteen Grand Slam titles. She also has three Olympic gold medals—one in singles and two in doubles.

Eldrick "Tiger" Woods (1975–) Tiger Woods is a pro golfer whose achievements to date already rank him among

Born in Cypress, Tiger Woods is among the most successful professional golf players of all time.

the most successful of all time. He's won fourteen major championships—the second highest of any male player—and sixty-five tour events for the Professional Golfers' Association of America (PGA). He has more major career wins and PGA Tour wins than any other active golfer. He is the youngest player to achieve the career Grand Slam, and the youngest and fastest player to win fifty tournaments on tour. According to estimates made by *Golf Digest* magazine, it is predicted that Woods will become the world's first professional athlete to earn $1 billion in winnings.

Science, Technology, and Industry

Charles P. Ginsburg (1920–1992) Charles Ginsburg was the leader of a research team at Ampex, an electronics company. He helped develop one of the first practical videotape recorders, which led to the creation of the video cassette recorder (VCR). Ginsburg was born in San Francisco.

Howard Hughes (1905–1976) Howard Hughes was an aviator, industrialist, film producer/director, philanthropist, and one of the wealthiest people in the world. He was born in Houston, Texas, but spent most of his adult life in and around Los Angeles. He gained fame in the late 1920s as a film producer, making big-budget movies like *Scarface* and *The Outlaw*. As an aviator, he set multiple world air-speed records and founded Hughes Aircraft Company. Eventually, he purchased Transworld Airlines (TWA).

Sally K. Ride (1951–) Sally Ride, born in Los Angeles, became the first American woman to enter outer space. She

A native of Los Angeles, Sally Ride became the first woman in space after she joined NASA as an astronaut.

earned two bachelor's degrees (in English and physics) and master's and doctoral degrees (both in physics) from Stanford University in Palo Alto. Ride joined the National Aeronautics and Space Administration (NASA) in 1978. On June 18, 1983, she entered space as a crew member aboard the Space Shuttle *Challenger*.

Timeline

1848	James Marshall discovers gold at Sutter's sawmill in Coloma. The discovery kicks off the gold rush of 1849, when hundreds of thousands of people migrated to California in hopes of striking gold and becoming rich.
1850	California is admitted into the Union as the thirty-first state.
1853	Levi Strauss invents blue jeans in San Francisco.
1906	A massive earthquake strikes San Francisco, resulting in fires that destroy more than 4.5 square miles (approximately 12 sq km) of the city.
1910	The first movie to be shot in Hollywood, *In Old California*, is filmed, marking the start of an industry that would make Hollywood the movie capital of the world.
1933	Dust storms begin to drive thousands of farming families from Oklahoma and the Plains states to California looking for agricultural work and a fresh start.
1937	The Golden Gate Bridge, spanning the Golden Gate Strait in San Francisco, opens.
1939	Bill Hewlett and David Packard found Hewlett-Packard in a Palo Alto garage, helping to establish Silicon Valley as the high-tech capital of the nation.
1967	Former actor Ronald Reagan is elected governor. The Summer of Love is declared, and thousands of hippies from throughout the United States descend upon San Francisco, particularly the Haight-Ashbury neighborhood.
1970	Student protests and riots rage on the University of California-Berkeley campus and Berkeley neighborhoods.
1989	A 7.1-magnitude earthquake hits the San Francisco Bay area, causing widespread damage, including the collapse of a double-decker portion of the Bay Bridge connecting San Francisco and Oakland.
2003	Actor and action movie star Arnold Schwarzenegger is elected governor.
2006	The California Global Warming Solutions Act establishes the first-ever comprehensive program of regulatory and market mechanisms to achieve real, measurable, cost-effective reductions of greenhouse gases.
2009	Protests erupt statewide in an attempt to overturn Proposition 8, a voter-approved ban on gay marriage.

California *at a Glance*

State motto	"Eureka." ("I have found it.")
State capital	Sacramento
State flower	California poppy
State bird	California quail
State tree	Redwood
Statehood date and number	1850, thirty-first state
State nickname	"The Golden State"
Total area and U.S. rank	163,696 square miles (423,971 sq km); third-largest state
Population	36,553,215
Length of coastline	840 miles (1,352 km)
Highest elevation	Mt. Whitney, at 14,495 feet (4,418 m)
Lowest elevation	Death Valley, at 282 feet (86 m) below sea level
Major rivers	Sacramento River, San Joaquin River, Colorado River
Major lakes	Lake Tahoe, Clear Lake, Mono Lake, Donner Lake

State Flag

State Seal

Hottest temperature recorded	134°F (57°C), at Death Valley, July 10, 1913
Coldest temperature recorded	-45°F (-43°C), in Boca, January 20, 1937
Origin of state name	The name "California" comes from a mythical Spanish island ruled by a queen named Califia who was featured in a Spanish romance. Spanish explorers originally thought California was an island.
Chief agricultural products	Milk, grapes, almonds, lettuce, strawberries, tomatoes, hay, oranges, broccoli, cotton, walnuts, rice, carrots, pistachios, lemons, avocados, wine
Major industries	Entertainment, aerospace, agriculture, computers, high tech

State Bird

State Flower

aqueduct A conduit for water.

blue state A U.S. state that tends to vote for Democratic Party candidates.

Cold War The state of conflict, tension, and competition that existed between the United States, the Soviet Union, and their respective allies from the mid-1940s to the early 1990s.

conglomerate A grouping of various companies under one large parent corporation.

Filipino The language spoken by those who originate from the country of the Philippines.

forty-niners A term used to describe the gold prospectors who came to California during the gold rush in 1849.

gold rush A massive influx of people who rushed to California in hopes of striking it rich after gold was discovered in the state.

hydroelectric power The production of power through the use of falling or flowing water.

impeachment The action of charging and trying a politician for criminal behavior or official misconduct.

independent filmmakers Those who make movies produced outside of the Hollywood studio system. Their films are usually called "indie films."

National Aeronautics and Space Administration (NASA) An agency of the U.S. government that is responsible for the nation's space program.

National Guard A reserve military force composed of state National Guard militia members or units.

silver screen Also known as a silver lenticular screen, this is a type of projection screen that was popular in the early years of the motion picture industry. It's still used in projecting 3-D films. The term "silver screen" has come to refer to the movies and the film industry in general.

Vietnam War The Vietnam War occurred in the countries of Vietnam, Laos, and Cambodia from 1959 to 1975. It was waged by Soviet-backed Communist North Vietnamese forces and U.S.-backed South Vietnamese and U.S. military personnel.

Academy of Motion Picture Arts and Sciences
8949 Wilshire Boulevard
Beverly Hills, CA 90211
(310) 247-3000
Web site: http://www.oscars.org

The Academy of Motion Picture Arts and Sciences is the world's preeminent movie-related organization. Its membership of more than six thousand of the most accomplished men and women in cinema votes to select the nominees and winners of the prestigious Academy Awards ("Oscars"), the highest recognition for work in the film industry.

Audubon California
765 University Avenue, Suite 200
Sacramento, CA 95825
(916) 649-7600
Web site: http://www.audubon-ca.org

Audubon California is an organization committed to building a better future for the citizens of California by protecting the state's outdoor treasures. It accomplishes this through conservation efforts, policy formation and advocacy, and educational outreach.

California Arts Council (CAC)
1300 I Street, Suite 930
Sacramento, CA 95814
(916) 322-6555
Web site: http://www.cac.ca.gov

The CAC encourages widespread public participation in the arts, helps build strong arts organizations at the local level, assists with the professional development of arts leaders, promotes awareness of the value of the arts, and directly supports arts programs for children and communities.

California Film Commission
7080 Hollywood Boulevard, Suite 900
Hollywood, CA 90028
(323) 860-2960
Web site: http://www.film.ca.gov

The California Film Commission enhances California's position as the leader in motion picture and television production. It can obtain filming permits, offers assistance on film productions and location scouting, and has a vast resource library for its members.

California State University (CSU)

401 Golden Shore

Long Beach, CA 90802

(562) 951-4000

Web site: http://www.calstate.edu

The CSU educational system has twenty-three campuses and enrolls more than 450,000 students. It is the largest university system in the United States.

California Tourism

P.O. Box 1499

Sacramento, CA 95812

(877) 225-4367

Web site: http://www.visitcalifornia.com

California Tourism's Web site features in-depth descriptions of various regions of the state, lists attractions and things to do, and provides tools that assist you in planning your trip to California.

Environment California

3435 Wilshire Boulevard, #385

Los Angeles, CA 90010

(213) 251-3688

Web site: http://www.environmentcalifornia.org

Environment California is a statewide, citizen-based environmental advocacy organization that fights to preserve and protect California's environment.

Web Sites

Due to the changing nature of Internet links, Rosen Publishing has developed an online list of Web sites related to the subject of this book. This site is updated regularly. Please use this link to access this list:

http://www.rosenlinks.com/uspp/capp

FOR FURTHER READING

Bishop, Greg, et al. *Weird California*. New York, NY: Sterling, 2006.

Elliott Bandini, Helen. *History of California: For Children*. Charleston, SC: Forgotten Books, 2008.

Lord, Rosemary. *Hollywood Then and Now*. Berkeley, CA: Thunder Bay Press, 2003.

Palm, Carl. *The Great California Story: Real-Life Roots of an American Legend*. Austin, TX: Northcross Books, 2004.

Starr, Kevin. *California: A History*. New York, NY: Modern Library, 2007.

Vlahides, John A. *Coastal California*. Footscray, Australia: Lonely Planet, 2007.

Williams, Gregory Paul. *The Story of Hollywood: An Illustrated History*. Los Angeles, CA: BL Press LLC, 2006.

Winokur, Jon. *The War Between the State: Northern California vs. Southern California*. Seattle, WA: Sasquatch Books, 2004.

BIBLIOGRAPHY

Brenneman, Richard. "The Bloody Beginnings of People's Park." *Berkeley Daily Planet*, April 20, 2004. Retrieved November 3, 2008 (http://www.berkeleydailyplanet.com/issue/2004-04-20/article/18700?status=301).

California.gov. "Early California History: An Overview." Retrieved November 3, 2008 (http://www.ca.gov).

California Historical Society. "California History Online." Retrieved December 1, 2008 (http://www.californiahistoricalsociety.org).

Chan, Sucheng, et al. *Major Problems in California History*. Boston, MA: Wadsworth Publishing, 1996.

Cherny, Robert, et al. *Competing Visions: A History of California*. New York, NY: Houghton Mifflin, 2000.

CityMayors.com. "The World's Largest Cities." Retrieved November 3, 2008 (http://www.citymayors.com/features/largest_cities1.html).

Cousins, Mark. *The Story of Film: A Worldwide History*. New York, NY: Thunder's Mouth Press, 2006.

Energy Information Administration. "California State Energy Profile." Retrieved November 5, 2008 (http://tonto.eia.doe.gov/state/state_energy_profiles.cfm?sid=CA).

King, Geoff. *New Hollywood Cinema: An Introduction*. New York, NY: Columbia University Press, 2002.

Legislative Analyst's Office. "Cal Facts 2006: California's Economy and Budget in Perspective." Retrieved November 13, 2008 (http://www.lao.ca.gov/2006/cal_facts/2006_calfacts_econ.htm).

Merchant, Carolyn. *Green Versus Gold: Sources in California's Environmental History*. Washington, DC: Island Press, 1998.

New York Times. "California's Legal Trouble." November 24, 2008. Retrieved November 26, 2008 (http://www.nytimes.com/2008/11/25/opinion/25tue4.html?_r=1&ref=opinion).

PBS.org. "The California Gold Rush." September 13, 2006. Retrieved November 9, 2008 (http://www.pbs.org/wgbh/amex/goldrush/peopleevents/e_goldrush.html).

Rawls, James J., and Walton Bean. *California: An Interpretive History*. New York, NY: McGraw Hill, 2006.

Sabato, Larry J. "Electoral Trends Warm Sunbelt, Freeze Frostbelt." CenterForPolitics.org, March 22, 2007. Retrieved November 3, 2008 (http://www.centerforpolitics.org/crystalball/article.php?id=LJS2007032201).

Smitha, Frank E. "The Sixties and Seventies from Berkeley to Woodstock." Retrieved November 8, 2008 (http://www.fsmitha.com/h2/ch28B.htm).

U.S. Census Bureau. "Population and Population Centers by State: 2000." November 10, 2005. Retrieved December 1, 2008 (http://www.census.gov/geo/www/cenpop/cntpop2k.html).

VisitCalifornia.com. "California History." Retrieved November 9, 2008 (http://www.visitcalifornia.com/AM/Template.cfm?Section=History).

INDEX

A

agriculture, 5, 8, 14, 25–26
animals, 12

C

California
  diversity of people in, 5, 30
  economy/industry of, 5, 8, 10, 15–17,
    25–29
  famous people from, 30–37
  geography of, 5, 6–12
  government of, 16, 20–24
  history of, 10, 13–19
  political influence of, 22, 24
  population of, 6, 16, 30
  as progressive/liberal state, 19, 22–24
Central Valley, 5, 8, 9, 26

E

entertainment industry, 15–17, 25, 27,
    31–33

F

forests, 5, 8, 12

G

glaciers, 11–12
gold rush, 5, 10, 14, 15, 16, 22, 28

H

Hearst, William Randolph, 32
Hewlett-Packard, 5, 27
Hollywood, 5, 16–17, 25

L

lakes, 7, 8–9
Los Angeles, 6, 14–15, 17
  history of, 10

M

Mexican-American War, 10, 14
Mexico, 6, 10, 13, 14
Mojave Desert, 11
mountains, 5, 6–8, 29
movie industry, 5, 15–17, 25, 27

N

Native Americans, 5, 13, 30

O

oil production, 10, 29

P

Pacific Ocean, 6, 9, 28
Pelosi, Nancy, 21
plants/trees, 5, 8, 12

R

railroads, 10, 14
Reagan, Ronald, 17–19
rivers, 9

S

Sacramento, 6, 20
San Francisco, 6, 14
San Francisco Bay, 9, 26, 28
Schwarzenegger, Arnold, 20
Sierra Nevada, 7, 8, 11, 15

Silicon Valley, 5, 26–28
student protests, 18

T

Tahoe, Lake, 7, 8
technology industry, 5, 25, 26–28
tourism, 8

water, war over, 14–15
wine production, 25, 28–29

Yosemite National Park, 8

About the Author

Laura La Bella is a writer residing in Rochester, New York. She has traveled throughout California, having visited Napa Valley, San Diego, San Francisco, Sacramento, and La Jolla. In 2000, La Bella ran the Rock n' Roll Marathon in San Diego to raise money for the Leukemia & Lymphoma Society.

Photo Credits

Cover, p. 1 (top left) Library of Congress Prints and Photographs Division; cover, p. 1 (top right) © Charles O'Rear/Corbis; cover (bottom) © www.istockphoto.com/Stas Volik; pp. 3, 6, 13, 20, 25, 30, 38 © www.istockphoto.com/Kenneth Sponster; p. 4 (top) © GeoAtlas; pp. 7, 23 © David McNew/Getty Images; p. 9 © www.istockphoto.com/Jay Spooner; p. 10 © The Granger Collection; p. 11 © J. Joyce/zefa/Corbis; p. 14 © www.istockphoto.com/Greg Panosian; p. 15 © www.istockphoto.com/Aaron Kohr; p. 17 © MPI/Getty Images; pp. 18, 26 © AP Photos; p. 21 © Robyn Beck/AFP/Getty Images; p. 28 © Scott Carson/Zuma Press; p. 29 © www.istockphoto.com; p. 31 © Trapper Frank/Corbis Sygma; p. 33 © Dirck Halstead/Time & Life Pictures/Getty Images; p. 35 © Donald Miralle/Getty Images; p. 37 © Bettmann/Corbis; p. 40 Wikimedia Commons.

Designer: Les Kanturek; Photo Researcher: Marty Levick